Hush, Child!
Can't You Hear the Music?

Hush, Child! Can't You Hear the Music?

Collected by Rose Thompson

Edited by Charles Beaumont

Foreword by John Stewart

A Brown Thrasher Original
The University of Georgia Press   Athens

143111

University of Georgia Press paperback edition, 1999
© 1982 by the University of Georgia Press
Athens, Georgia 30602
All rights reserved

Set in 12 on 14 point Cheltenham
Designed by Sandra Strother Hudson
The paper in this book meets the guidelines for
permanence and durability of the Committee on
Production Guidelines for Book Longevity of the
Council on Library Resources.

Printed in the United States of America
03 02 01 00 99 P 5 4 3 2 1

The Library of Congress has cataloged the cloth edition of this book as follows:
Library of Congress Cataloging in Publication Data
Main entry under title:
Hush, child! can't you hear the music?
"A Brown Thrasher original."
1. Afro-American folk-lore—Georgia. 2. Georgia—Social life and customs.
3. United States. Farm Security Administration.
I. Thompson, Rose. II. Beaumont, Charles Allen.
GR111.A47H87 398.2'09758 81-10442
ISBN 0-8203-0588-X (alk. paper)
ISBN 0-8203-2137-0 (pbk. : alk. paper)
AACR2

Nearly all the photographs in this book were taken in Greene County, Georgia,
in the late 1930s and early 1940s. Most of them were taken by Rose Thompson.
Those on pages xxi, xxiv–xxv, xxxiv–1, 30–31, 56–57, and 93 were taken by
Jack Delano, a Farm Security Administration photographer.

for Mary Virginia

Contents

Sound the Trumpet

Preface

The Countess used to take lunch at the coffee shop of the old Georgian Hotel in Athens in 1950. My friends and I would walk up from the university and dine there too. We would see this handsome woman of such grace and style that we called her "The Polish Countess." Her style was both of attire and of manner. The next year I went to see about renting a garage apartment in Five Points in Athens. The little building had two apartments over three garages. The tenant of the one I was to rent was not at home, so my prospective landlord took me to see the other one, occupied by a Miss Thompson, the visiting teacher for the Clarke County Schools. The door opened and there stood the Polish Countess. Her rich, southern speech belied our name for her, but we still sometimes call her the Countess. As I left, she said, "If you rent the apartment, I'll share my mint bed with you."

Over subsequent mint juleps, our friendship developed. She was full of wonderful stories about her family and her friends, told with a keen self-deprecating wit. I soon learned that my new neighbor had, during the 1930s and 1940s, collected black folklore while working in middle Georgia. Although not trained as a folklorist with tape-recorder, she had such a profound interest in and love for the people she interviewed that she was determined to capture their stories on paper. She developed her own shorthand, consisting mainly of key letters and dashes (k- ltrs, f. ex.). She says that she had to transcribe her notes soon or lose much of what she had gathered.

Her collection of black folklore is important not only for the beauty and music she caught but also for her having interviewed blacks who were, for the most part, old even in those decades, the last of the generation who knew these stories. Had it not been for Rose, this part of their culture could have been lost.

While working on a survey of old structures for the State of Georgia, Department of Human Resources, Patricia Cooper discovered Rose's home near White Plains. While chatting about her 1900-vintage farmhouse, Rose talked of her stories too. Mrs. Cooper became interested and arranged for us to send them to Eliot Wigginton to consider for *Foxfire* magazine. Subsequently Eliot and Marty Henderson, a student writer from Rabun County High School, met Rose at my house. Marty and Eliot chose about a dozen and published them, with an interview, in the Winter 1977 edition of *Foxfire* magazine. We thank Eliot for his permission to reprint those stories here.

I suppose that Rose's Ancient Mariner need to talk about these stories has rubbed off onto me, for when I was congratulating Iris Hill on the University of Georgia Press's new Brown Thrasher series, I fell to talking about Rose's stories. The result is this book.

I taped about eight hours of interviews with Rose over a period of several months. From these tapes I have developed the single composite interview into which we have placed the stories as Rose's comments lead into them.

Rose and I wish to thank, in addition to Eliot Wigginton and Patricia Cooper, Connell W. Smith for her early help and interest, Joy Morris for typing, and Katherine K. Scott for her support.

Charles Beaumont

Foreword

When Rose Thompson did her collecting of black American folklore in the 1930s and 1940s, black Americans were well into a substantive drifting away from their traditional lore as a standard by which moral and social behavior should be assessed and wit cultivated. As the freedmen and their generations drifted away from the rural plantations, as they entered the cities of the North and South seeking new ways to make a living, they experienced likewise an emotional and spiritual migration, which would demand new ways of seeing the world and their place in it. Consequently, these days, black Americans rely less on the old lore than on written historical and sociological texts for a communal ideology. This is in keeping with being a twentieth-century people in a modern industrial culture. But dis-use as a communal tool is no sign that traditional black American lore has lost its value.

In neighborhood meeting places, in bars, in work-places where work may be accompanied by the telling voice, black Americans continue to tell each other about themselves, about their escapades and tall feats, about the terrors and seductions through which they have acquired new knowledge. The situations may be neither cosmic nor mythological, and the leading characters may have everyday instead of biblical names. The plots and themes may be thinly veiled historical issues too. But the resonances and the resolutions, where one comes upon such a telling, echo the old stories just as clearly, and perhaps it is after all true that wisdom endures even as the generations change.

So that in a Gloucester Street bar in Brunswick, Georgia, one overhears: *Fellow once got trapped in ——— but managed to slip into a hiding place and elude the mob. After dark he was trying to leave town, and ended up crawling across the trestle of a bridge. Suddenly he came up on a rattlesnake. The snake immediately coiled and rattled. In desperation, the fellow reached for a stick and he was about to beat that snake to death when it said, "Stop man! Don't hit me. I'm trying to get out of town too. . . ." And if you think that was mean, back in ——— they hardly allowed blacks on the street after five o'clock in the evening, and worse than that, black people couldn't laugh on the streets either. If they were in town and just had to laugh, they had to go to a special barrel on the corner and put their heads down inside that barrel and laugh in there. And every Monday morning they would take that barrel and empty it in the river, and you used to hear all those laughs, ha ha ha, heh heh heh, going down the river. Every Monday morning. . . .*

The sentiments expressed in these vignettes are not new, even if the code of the pieces themselves is less obscure. And the pattern of communicating insight through exaggerated metaphor remains intact and strong. Perhaps in time, when these new storytellers become old and gray, someone like Rose Thompson will come along to take down their distilled tales and experiences, their version of the old wisdom. Such collections, as this one clearly demonstrates, can be a viable testimony to the stamina and flexibility of which human beings are capable.

In the first part of this collection we meet Mr. Rabbit and the Devil. Both of these are familiar characters in black American folklore from the traditional period. Mr. Rabbit is the American cousin of Mr. Spider, the West African Anansi. He is a mischievous and skillful manipulator, and to be dealt with warily. Mr. Rabbit, he will fool you with his mundane ways, but he can dance. And if you aren't careful in dealing with him, he will whip you too, and lord it over you. The Devil, he roams the world encouraging people not to do right. He will fool and manipulate you too, and he is not only mischievous, he's malevolent. Rabbit and Devil are masters of disguise and misdirection, and often get their way. But they can be outdone if one has faith, unshakable faith, and a careful suspicion of outward appearances.

In the second part of the collection we encounter *the charmed place,* a staple in all lores coming out of peasant traditions. We encounter too the powerfully gifted individual in a tale that echoes the story of the Greek Orpheus, whose music could make gods and devils obey. Only in this case, the gift is used to overcome the Devil. We see in this section, as well, evidence of the power of religion. In the last part of *Hush, Child! Can't You Hear the Music?* the power of religion is a sustained theme not only in word and idea but in song,

and what had been an understated rhythm—perhaps inten-
tion—of the book blossoms out into a full celebration of the
ways and strengths of the Lord, the musical power through
which he may be invoked in any emergency.

There is instruction here in the grand folk manner on how
to meet and survive the ever-present stress in the lives of the
folk. And much of that instruction is coded in the running
dialogue between Rose Thompson and Charles Beaumont
which holds the tales and experiences together. In fact, their
encounter, as it is told, is a mixture of imagination and ro-
mance quite, in itself, characteristic of folk behavior. And the
grace that may be achieved in the sharing of an empathetic
relationship with others comes across clearly all through
their exchange. Their dialogue establishes an appropriate
distance between the emotional and intellectual experience
of the lore itself. The quiet tone of analysis and explanation
achieved here is one of the strongest attributes of the total
work.

There are some instances in which the overview runs thin,
and Rose Thompson, out of a wish not to be regarded as
someone special, one could believe, makes light of the schol-
arly tradition into which her work might fit. But she has managed to achieve a very special task in the portraits of her
storytellers. We get a keen sense of who these storytellers
were, and how they meant their stories to be taken. These
portraits are together an exegesis as eloquent as any that
might accompany a collection such as this.

Subtly communicated, too, is a caution against the too
hurried dismissal of the imagination as a faculty on which

human beings may rely in meeting situations of stress and crisis. The obvious play between reality and fabrication makes clear the responsibility taken on by the folk communicators for keeping alive the sense that the world is fashioned as we recognize and cultivate certain images among ourselves.

Thompson and Beaumont are to be commended for this contribution to the store of letters which, although drawn from the lives and culture of black Americans, stands as a legacy for all Americans who are unafraid of accepting their total history. It deserves the widest reading.

John Stewart

Introduction

In the gently rolling hills of middle Georgia, Rose Thompson was born about the turn of the century. This section has continued to be her home, as it was also for most of the blacks she interviewed. Her birthplace, Liberty Church community, is now inundated by Lake Sinclair.

She was steeped in family storytelling, especially the tales her father told her, stories his father had told his family. She also heard the stories of her Aunt Pat, whom you will meet later in this book. You will also meet some of the blacks whom Rose grew up knowing and listening to. She recalls more of her father's ironic manner of delivery of accounts of real events than she does particular stories, most of which were Irish. He told of a young girl who was upstairs in her Irish farmhouse dressing to meet the young man downstairs who was asking for her hand in marriage. The attic floor was not solidly nailed. She made a misstep and fell, incompletely clothed, right into the young man's lap. Her unabashed father said, "Girl, split to the fodder stack." Rose says that when she was a little girl and got herself into an embarrassing situation, a frequent occurrence, her father would say, "Rose, split to the fodder stack." Whether a person arrived by car or by

Rose Thompson

horseback, his welcome (if he wanted the person to stay) was "Lite and look at your saddle." It was a household of stories and recurring phrases from old stories reapplied to passing situations.

Rose's early schooling was in White Plains at the now defunct Dawson Institute and Georgia Normal Industrial College. Later she attended Georgia State College for Women at Milledgeville. Her first jobs were in Atlanta; at Howell Mill Road Grammar School for a year, then Liberty Guinn Grammar School. One of her brothers was Assistant Superintendent of Banks for the state and lived in Atlanta. Perhaps because she wanted more independence from him, or from the boardinghouse where they both lived, she moved to Sandersville, where she taught the third grade for two years. This brought her nearer the locale of these stories. In 1932 Rose taught in a Columbus, Georgia, mill school, sponsored by the Bibb Manufacturing Company and the school board.

Rose also worked in the nursery school of the old Union School of Athens, an academy for black students. Rose's main career was as a home supervisor for the Farm Security Administration, and it was this work that brought her close to the people who gave her these stories. This background in education, however, was useful when the Second World War caused FSA supervisors to give more time to the community. Rose taught in the Georgia State College for Women (now Georgia College at Milledgeville). She worked in the nursery school there. When the FSA wanted to transfer her to a county in South Georgia where she would be both farm and home supervisor, she resigned. That autumn (1944) she taught a course in rural problems at Georgia State College for Women. But to too many of her friends and clients in the county she was still "the government lady," who could repair the pressure cooker or untangle snarled red-tape. There was not enough time. So Rose returned to Athens for graduate work in education, beyond the M.A. in English she had received in 1931. Subsequently she became visiting teacher for Clarke County, Georgia. In this job she guided parents and teachers to the agency or service that could best help the child who was having a problem.

Before I describe Rose's work with the Farm Security Administration, some background of the depression years in middle Georgia will help us see both the plight of the people who gave Rose most of these stories and the work Rose did to help them. The land and the people of this section experienced an odd, changed sameness after the Civil War: for the most part, the same owners had the land and the same fieldhands worked it. The former slaves became hired fieldhands, and sharecropping began, a practice in which the landowner supplied the tenant farmer with all of his needs in return for the yield minus the tenant's small share for his labor.

The Civil War had not destroyed the plantation as a block of land to be worked, but the depression of the 1870s hastened the breakup of the plantation. By the turn of the century more and more land was sold off or was in the receivership of insurance companies and banks, who in turn became the usually impersonal agent for the sharecropper to deal with. This trend coincided with the nationwide depression of the 1890s. So many blacks were out of work that they fell prey to unscrupulous traders in migrant workers. The infamous R. A. Williams, called "Peg-leg" Williams, induced (seduced?) thousands of blacks to allow him to transport them to the Mississippi Delta, where he advertised his product in the papers for the Delta planters to see. Arthur F. Raper, in his *Tenants of the Almighty* (New York: Macmillan, 1943, p. 132), quotes the Augusta *Chronicle* for January 14, 1900: "It is clear that fully 2,500 have gone from Morgan and 1,500 to 2,000 from Greene."

Because the smaller landowners were under the same economic pressures, they too after the depression of the

xx

1890s and the Great Depression of the 1930s lost much of their land through mortgages and borrowing from local merchants who had advanced supplies. Thus, like the insurance companies, local merchants inadvertently became holders of land to be sharecropped. This is not to suggest that some large and many small farmers did not survive and maintain the family farm; it is to show the general climate of work and life that most of the blacks Rose interviewed had endured.

> Wish I was dead;
> Wish I was rotten.
> Wish my bones
> Was as white as cotton.

Rose found this rime from slavery times in Baldwin County. One wonders how far into the twentieth century blacks, on the bottom of a ruined system, were still singing this bitter tune.

With the advent of Franklin Roosevelt's administration in 1932 the federal government began a broad medley of programs designed to alleviate many of the problems I have described. For the people there were the Child Health and Welfare Program; the Civilian Conservation Corps, which organized young men into work groups for land and forest reclamation; the Old Age Assistance Act, which gave monthly financial help to those who could not work; the Surplus Commodities program, which doled out food already purchased by the government to bolster farmers' prices; the National Youth Administration, which helped some high school and college students financially.

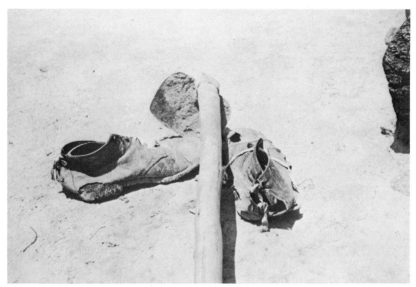

A Weary Day in the Field

Other programs helped both the people and the land: the Agriculture Adjustment Administration, under which farmers willing to limit production and cooperate in soil rebuilding measures were given money grants; the Soil Conservation Service, which was the arm of AAA for its second objective and which helped organize black and white farmers into Soil Conservation Districts; the Rural Electrification Administration, which sought to create electricity from new dams and deliver it to farm families on a new network of lines; the Farm Credit Administration; the Rural Rehabilitation Program, which advanced money to tenants to purchase the land they had been sharecropping and which advanced money to the

Mother and Son, Greene County, Georgia, 1941

Washday

tenant or the landlord for improvement of houses and barns, the money being repaid from future rents signed over by the landlord.

Many of these programs were administered by or co-ordinated locally by the Farm Security Administration. Rose Thompson and her sister Ruby Thompson worked in many of these programs during their tenures in FSA. Before she became associated with FSA, Ruby had been the first home demonstration agent for Greene County under the Georgia

Extension Service. FSA had farm supervisors (men) to deal with farming and land matters and home supervisors (women) to deal with kitchen gardening, food preservation, vocational rehabilitation—the general improvement of the quality of farm life. These supervisors delivered information to the people for whom this vast network of much of the alphabet had been created. Rose said that a lady in Eatonton said that if you saw a stray on the street, it was probably a government worker. Rose assumes that she was such a stray.

As home supervisor Rose encouraged farm wives (both tenants and small-farm owners) to create or enlarge vegetable gardens and learn to sustain winter gardens. She taught them how to use the new pressure cookers, which many called "precious cookers," more through wit than ignorance, one suspects. These families were encouraged to can so many jars per crop per person and to preserve so much meat, mainly pork and beef, per person. She showed them how to make homemade chick brooders. They also learned how to make mattresses and soft yellow creamed cheese. Rose brought them new recipes from the Extension Service of the State Department of Agriculture.

Rose's innate tact and skill in getting these stories aided her, I'm sure, in her work with these people. She became a friend who was there, who could be relied on, and whom they knew they could call on. As Rose puts it, "You don't just go out and say, 'I know everything and you know so little.' They already know a lot, and you take what they already know and show them some easier, better ways." Rose says that if a good gardener asked her how to raise tomatoes, she would say,

"Tell me how you raised these; they are as good as I have seen." He would be pleased, and maybe she could then help him in some other way. She could also go home and do her tomatoes that way and pass along his ideas to another farmer.

Usually Rose asked one or two of her clients to help her with instruction at a called group meeting. There was no regular club with fixed meetings. She knew enough people in an area to pass the word along to announce a meeting. Sometimes, too, local civic clubs like Rotary would ask her to speak. Once she spoke on WSB radio in Atlanta on how to

make the soft yellow creamed cheese. Another time she took a tenant purchaser with her to WSB to talk on gardening.

I must confess that I am always amazed that Rose did all of these things, for I find her so unaggressive and unbossy. She was frying chicken that first time I met her, and I have never known her to cook since. She seems to manage on foods that take little preparation. Once she wanted to have a few of us in for supper but did not want to cook. I suggested she have pizza brought in. This was in the "tree house," her name for the garage apartments. Well, the party was not very interesting and, downcast, Rose chided me the next day: "Anyway, why didn't you tell me that pizza is nothing but hoecake with a little cheese on it?" I am sure that what made Rose such a success in her work and in collecting these stories is her immediate warmth and wit, a genuineness so apparent that you know not only that you want to accept her but that you can trust her. It is the same quality which later in this book she attributes to Aunt Millie, who told her three of these stories. Even when a bill collector would try to use her to find an elusive debtor, Rose would not allow herself to be so used. She was welcomed where others were not.

This central part of her character admitted her into people's lives and her quick ear allowed her to hear the music of their stories. Robert Penn Warren, writing of Eudora Welty in the *New York Times Book Review* of March 12, 1980, observes that there is "a special kind of conversational flow among Southern women—or at least a remarkable plenty of them" that contributes to the literature of such writers as Eudora Welty, Katherine Anne Porter, Flannery O'Connor, and

Caroline Gordon. He continues, "This was not ordinary gossip (although gossip no doubt thrived) but gossip providing the tale for its own sake, sad and humorous: the character sketch, the narrative, grotesque, comic or poetic description; gusts of feeling, delicate ironies and small, acute observations, bright as a needle point—all things that characterize 'women's talk,' which is somehow different from a man's tale, even when it is itself a tale. This kind of woman's talk knows no class—though it naturally differs from class to class in its concerns and tone." Although not yet a practicing writer, Rose is a practicing talker and listener and I believe that she has some of the qualities Warren characterizes.

Rose has found that "the blacks are the ones who said the clever things. And as I worked with them I felt more at ease with them. I knew that they accepted me completely and I accepted them. They knew that they could be entertaining and that I wanted to be entertained by their stories. I was relaxed, usually off the highway a piece. There was nothing much to bother you. You could hear the birds singing. Maybe somebody singing way off. It was a relaxed situation and the blacks would delve back into things they had heard, and said them without thinking, I think, just like a bird would. But the white people didn't know the things the blacks knew. They don't till this day. White people have stories that go around, but they are not as tellable, if that's a good word. And these stories sort of get hold of you; you don't forget them."

Rose has a sure sense for the story; she has too this feeling for the music of it. Having studied violin at the old Atlanta Conservatory of Music, Rose has a keen ear for the lilt of the

Dinnertime at Liddy Purify's

vernacular. As she puts it, "I have that feeling for music and I believe that is one reason I wrote prose like it is, to get some of that feeling of music out of me, why I love the old stories so; from them I get a sort of echo of music that I wanted to produce myself." When she heard the old man telling how Michael had defeated Lucifer in the battle in Heaven and had thrown Lucifer "over the bannister of time," she simply and uniquely heard the music of that phrase and set it down. Just so, the old man telling her the story of Fiddlers Mountain and the magic music there: "Hush, child! Can't you hear the music?" Rose could.

In addition to her skill in hearing collectable stories, Rose also heard the stray comment of humor and folk wisdom. The sadness of the old woman's complaint, "My longest days are over" and "I can't remember old times so good; done got so old and painful." The humor of Tom Lattimer's comment on his tumbled-down house: "This is my summer house." The wry wisdom of "If you want to keep out of trouble, keep your eyes and ears open and your mouth and door shut." And "More marries than thrives." And "Charge it to the dust and let the rain settle it." The determination of Jim Reed: "If I ain't got but a dime, I'm going to spend it on something to eat; I'm not going to be here long and I ain't going to stay here hungry. If you eat, you can walk strong; if you don't eat, you can't walk at all." Of James Butts's self-knowledge: "I have made good money, but I have such a lending heart that I can't keep much. Some folks are too lending with their lives." Of a thank-you-mam bucket: "If you work for somebody and they give you something to take things home in,

Tom Lattimer and His "Summer House"

that's your thank-you-mam bucket. If you crook your arm to hang it on, you are toting a crooked arm. Some will say, 'I don't tote no crooked arm.'" Of wasting one's time: "Well, Lord, this ain't doing me. Let me get away from here." Of intentional metaphor: "Barefoot coffee is coffee without sugar and cream; without cream is without stockings; without sugar is without shoes." Of unintentional misuse of words: "Before my house burned up, I was in as nice a fix as any folks would want to be." Of concealing one's age: "I'm old enough to ramble, too young to settle down." And, finally, of history: "The world go so fast you can't keep nothing on your mind unless you got it writ down." And Rose wrote a vital part of it down.

Over the
Bannister of
Time

Rose: *I was driving home to White Plains from Milledgeville one Friday—it must have been in 1945—and I noticed a very old black man sitting in the yard way off the highway on a dirt road. When I got closer I could see that he was shelling peas. We introduced ourselves. He was Uncle Wright Boyer. This was in Hancock County. I told him that I would like to hear some stories of the old times. "How old?" "As far back as you can go." "I can go all the way back to the Devil. Is that far enough for you?" I told him it was. He said that my writing it down would not bother him. Every once in a while he would pause and say, "Now, read me what you done writ."*

The Devil

The Devil was plenty smart back in the old days, and bless your time, he was one of the greatest songsters in heaven. Surely was. He used to lead the singing choir up there in heaven and sometime he would hop up on a pole and whistle just like a mockingbird. There just wasn't any stopping him.

Wright Boyer

He used to issue out the blessing three times a day amongst the other angels up there, and he named himself Champion Luther. If ever there was a sight, he was one.

Then he got to cutting up powerful bad; said if he didn't take that kingdom, he was going to build a kingdom to the north side of that one about a span above the stars. And that proves it was a starry heaven. Um-m-m-hum! Um-m-m-hum!

Well, then, after he had done all that talking, he up and banished himself. After a while Michael was standing by the Royal where God was seated and he looked out and saw the Devil coming back and he said, "Behold! The great dragon is coming to take vengeance on our kingdom, all-stained-in-hallowed-blood."

And when he got there the Devil raised a war. He fought and cut up scandalous and backed the angels up under the throne. God was sitting there watching from the Royal.

And then the Devil disappeared again. And when he had come back Michael looked out and saw him again. And he said, "Be-HO-O-OLD! The great dragon is a coming again!"

God didn't say anything to Michael the other time, but this time He said, "Michael, you go out and meet him and put him out of here. If you have to reach back there in my wardrobe and take seven bolts of thunder and put against him. Put him out of here, Michael! Put him out!"

God was just sitting on the Royal watching to see what was going to happen. Michael grabbed the Devil and the Lord told him to put him out. Michael threw the Devil over the bannister of time. Then he tipped over and peeped way down and saw the Devil where he had dropped to and he said, "Lord, the great dragon fell way down to torment."

Then the Lord said, "Michael, hurry right on down and beat the Devil to earth, and chain him tight and fast." And that is what Michael did and the Devil has been chained ever since.

You say you believe it—you might as well too, for it is written in the Bible for you to read.

Rose spent some of the summer of 1946 in Clayton, in Rabun County, Georgia, where she understood few blacks lived. But with her usual curiosity she discovered the teller of one of her most artistic stories, "Fiddlers Mountain." Many double-ridged mountaintops look like fiddles lying on their sides and are therefore called Fiddlers Mountain, and Rose's storyteller may have chosen a north Georgia peak for the locale of the story. There is not, however, a mountain visible from Clayton by that name, although this characteristic shape occurs. When this story was published in Foxfire *magazine, the editors tried to find some trace or memory of the old preacher who related the tale to Rose, but they were unsuccessful. He was quite old in 1946 and seemed to Rose not to have had a congregation.*

Rose: *I had heard that there were very few blacks in Rabun County, and I knew better than just to go rambling around. So I asked someone at the courthouse if it would be all right for me to go up there, and that person showed me the way to where an old black woman lived. She was nice enough about it, but she was a little vague about why she thought they called it Fiddlers Mountain. But she said the Reverend over there, he lived around a bend in the road, would know. She sent for the preacher, and sure enough he could tell and they then told it together although the preacher did most of the talking.*

5

The Reverend

Fiddlers Mountain

Why do they call it Fiddlers Mountain? Because nothing lives on it except those two musicians—just a fiddling and a swaying as they sit there and play. Any moonshiny night you can see them just a pulling the bow; and if you listen with a keen ear and a fearful heart, you can hear their music.

Bless your time, nobody knows how long they have been sitting there, but they are playing yet—to be sure. It was too long ago that a man came to one of the fiddlers and asked him to play the fiddle for him that night. Come to such and such a mountain. Going to be a big ball. And when night came, the fiddler went up on that mountain and took another man with him.

6

And when they got up on the mountain there, they saw a great big house. Carriages and horses standing around. House all lit up. Laughing and talking going on—men and women all dressed up; women with trail train dresses on. Gave the fiddlers a seat and they went to playing. Every time they went through a cotillion, would come and pay the fiddlers. What a time they had! And just about that time the old Devil pranced in all dressed up and took his seat. They were all dancing and a bold gal walked up to the Devil and asked him to be her partner.

Devil got up and bowed and scraped and led the gal out in the ring. Then he set in to dance. He danced and danced. Cut so many capers that he pretty near danced that poor gal to death. Folks commenced to look at him and saw he had a pewter eye. After a while he cut so many fancy steps, they saw he had a club foot. All quit dancing. But the Devil kept on and danced the gal plumb to death. All the folks fell down on their knees, and the Devil went out and took the side of the house with him—a braying like a mule.

And when the clock struck twelve, house went out of existence. House disapppeared. House went down like a light going out. Nothing left but the two musicians still sitting up there on the mountain—just a fiddling and a swaying.

Hush, child! Can't you hear the music?

Rose: *Now, you should have known Uncle Bob Watkins. He had a real gift for a story. He worked for my father and used to groom my horse Jezebel, a little sorrel mare with a pretty*

Bob Watkins

mane. One morning Bob came in very excited, and he didn't often get excited, but he said that every bit of her mane had been plaited in little plaits. I asked him who had done this, and he said, "Nobody ain't done it. The witches rid her last night." I didn't dispute it; I didn't know.

Charles: *Seems to me there is a tradition of fairies plaiting horses' manes.*

Rose: *I don't know, but I don't believe that Bob plaited Jezebel's. There were so many of them and they were so tiny. One reason I told you that story was that I always had the feeling that Uncle Bob could see and hear things other folks couldn't. At any rate, as I just about believed Uncle Bob's story of Jezebel's mane, I began to believe his story about the rabbit dance, knowing what a prankster a rabbit can be, to say nothing of cats as mighty hunters.*

Rabbit Dance

Was a moonshiny night in a sandbed: dance there because it was soft to their foots. They dance the six-hand reel set, the rabbits did—or maybe it was the eight-hand reel, I saw that! Them rabbits dancing, all dressed up with frocktail coats and high top hats. Of course there was boy rabbits and girl rabbits. Of course there was. . . .

Swing on the corners—that they did. Then one was calling the sets. It's the truth, a rabbit dances. Them creatures dance all night: standing on their hind foots, joining hands, and stomping around. They swing on the corners and promenade all! Go down and dance with the foot gentleman, sashay to the right, and balance to the left. Going round and round.

Lord, yes—they dances—rabbits does.

Cut such fancy capers because they're so little and light, I reckon.

Or they used to do it—don't know what them critters is up to now.

But just go out to a sandbed some moonshiny night; plenty rabbits travel then. Rabbit has got a heap of sense, and is surely going to ramble around. And, Lawsy, such music—had to have music to dance by. There was a banjo-picking rabbit: set up in the corner of the fence patting his foots and a knocking that banjo, and his hat set on the back of his head.

Rabbits always cutting capers: believe they used to be folks. Done got off in the woods and act like they wild.

But, them creatures can dance!

Rose: *Uncle Bob played an important part in my life; he worked around our house for many years and his wife, Lila, cooked there. Bob kept several kinds of wood on the woodpile. He would burn oak and hickory on weekdays, but on Sunday mornings he would lay the fire with white wood like ash. He said that would be showing respect for the day. Also on Sundays, he would pull out the lighter-colored hay for the animals in the barn. His wife, Lila, was a good cook. We had a little old train that ran right by here. It would go up to Union Point in the morning, come back at dinner, go back up in the*

Lila Watkins

afternoon. It was a branch of the Georgia Railroad. That train would pass here at 11:30 every morning and Aunt Lila would talk to the train: "I hear you; I got my bread on. You needn't be blowing at me."

Charles: *Is Uncle Bob the man who got rid of the polecats?*

Rose: *No, that was Ma Mary's husband, Jim Moore, the man who said that he didn't believe in hants. He was coming from town one night in his wagon, with nothing in it, but it got so heavy that the mule couldn't pull it. He had been bragging that he didn't believe in hants and there were some hants*

11

in his wagon, and he said that one of them nearly slapped his head off. That's what he said.

Charles: *But what about the polecats?*

Rose: *A family of polecats had taken up residence in our woodpile. Pa-Jim (that's what we called my father when we didn't call him the Major) got Jim Moore to come over with his dogs and clean them out. The dogs ran most of them away, but Jim shot one and hung it up on a tree limb. His dogs kept barking at it, and Jim said to his dogs, "You better come on and leave them white folk's polecat alone."*

Charles: *Did he think the whites that possessive?*

Rose: *May be.*

Rose: *Eli Rittenberry of Greene County told me this story. He was honest enough to say that he did not entirely believe it. Before he told it, he talked a while about cats. He said, "Cats are strange creatures and you can't understand their ways. A cat can look deep into your eyes, but you cannot look into a cat's eyes: you can look at them, but not into them." He described a cat's eye as somewhat like a small glass marble, without depth.*

Cats Toting a Cat

Once there was an old man going home one night just before dark and he met some cats toting a cat. Those cats stopped the old man and said, "Old man, when you get home you tell your old woman that Sis Cahline is dead."

Eli Rittenberry

This worried the old man for he didn't understand about those cats a-talking. But he went on home and there was his old woman putting on a hoe-cake of bread in a spider in front of the fire. He never thought that the cats were her own kind, so he said, "I just met some cats toting a cat and they said to tell your old woman that Sis Cahline is dead."

And that old woman jumped up and holloed right loud, "Bless God—Sis Cahline is dead!"

And then she greased herself all over right quick with buzzard grease, slipped her skin off and turned into a cat, and jumped in the spider of bread and whizzed right up the chimney.

Now the old man had always said if his old woman ever turned to a witch, he was going to quit her right then and there. So he got his hat and left and nobody has ever seen him from that day to this.

Rose: *Jolie told me the story of "Aunt Tucky-de-Dandy." Jolie was a sight. At the end of the story, Jolie would say, "I don't know Aunt Tucky-de-Dandy; I don't know Aunt Tucky-de-Dandy," accenting the know, but all rather softly. She said that in a sort of chant. When we were children and got into a situation we couldn't handle, we'd say, "Skinny, don't you know me? Don't you know me, Skinny?" Miss Pat told us that story, but when I was grown Jolie told it too. Jolie told it with much more drama and order.*

Aunt Tucky-de-Dandy

One time there was an old woman that used to turn to a witch and jump out of her skin and then go wandering "breviting" around.

One morning she told her children that she was going off a piece and if anybody asked about her to say:

14

Don't know Aunt Tucky-de-Dandy,
Don't know Aunt Tucky-de-Dandy.
Then she slipped out of her skin right quick and hung it behind the back door on a nail. And then that old woman disappeared right before their eyes.

And whensomever anybody knocked on the door and asked about the old woman, all of the children would say:

Don't know Aunt Tucky-de-Dandy,
Don't know Aunt Tucky-de-Dandy.
But after a while that old woman thought she better go home and get inside her skin.

But, law me child, while she had been gone, somebody had put a whole passel of salt inside her skin. No matter how hard she tried, she just couldn't get inside of it again.

After a while she got worried and said right easy:

Skinny, Skinny, don't you know me?
Skinny, don't you know me?
And the skin said right back to the old woman:

Don't know Aunt Tucky-de-Dandy,
No Ma'am, don't know Aunt Tucky-de-Dandy.
The old woman kept on working to get inside her skin, and she begged right pitiful like:

Skinny, Skinny, this is me,
Don't you know me, Skinny?
And everytime the skin would say:

Don't know Aunt Tucky-de-Dandy.
Then the old woman got so scared that she ran out of the house. She ran and ran until she came to the creek. She

jumped in head and ears; and time she went under the water, the frogs started saying right loud:

Don't know Aunt Tucky-de-Dandy, de-Dandy, de-Dandy.

Then they started saying it right easy:

Don't know Aunt Tucky-de-Dandy,

Don't know Aunt Tucky-de-Dandy.

And they are still saying that same thing. You've heard them many a time.

Charles: *What else do you know about Jolie?*

Rose: *She was a naughty old woman. She sang me this song:*

> *Went down the road to the shufly's house.*
> *Shufly warn't at home.*
> *Got in bed with the shufly's wife.*
> *Stay till the shufly come home.*

> *Went down the road to the buzzard's house.*
> *Buzzard warn't at home.*
> *Got in bed with the buzzard's wife.*
> *Stay till the buzzard come home.*

I don't think that there was any spiritual side to her. She didn't think of anything ethereal.

> *Old man, old man, I want your daughter.*
> *She's upstairs. You can have her for a quarter.*

17

That's another one of Jolie's rhymes. She had several husbands. She was interesting and lively. I liked to talk with her. She worked several years in New York City. She said she worked on Millionary Road; never worked for no poor folks. She was an exaggerator; she had a good imagination. Jolie told me once about this old man, I think he was kin to her, and he had this old mule he rode all the time. The man would get so drunk that he would almost fall off the right side of the mule. The mule knew it, and he would go on down the left side so he could get the man safely home. Jolie was a sight. And fun-loving.

Charles: *Where did you get the story about Old Lady Mary and the heifer shoes?*

Rose: *I got that in Greene County. I just happened to hear that Old Lady Mary was a good storyteller.*

Charles: *People know that you are looking for stories so they tell you?*

Rose: *Yes, they tell me where to go.*

Charles: *What's her full name?*

Rose: *Old Lady Mary Jones. She lived between White Plains and Siloam, on a through road but not one of the paved roads. It was back; but I knew where she lived. She knew the Thompsons, but she didn't know me.*

Charles: *That name could get you into a lot of houses.*

Rose: *That's right. She said, "Your dad must be Mr. Jimmy Thompson; then you got a brother named Mr. Jimmy Thompson." Yes, that helped me a lot to get into places. Well, I told her that I just wanted to talk about the old times, that I knew that she had known of lot of old people.*

18

Charles: *How old was she?*
Rose: *She was about seventy-five.*
Charles: *Can you remember when you got this story?*
Rose: *It was about 1947. So I had heard that she saw the funny side of life, the comical, and that some of these stories that she told probably were not true and that she might have added to what she had heard, or that some of the stories that went around among them you get different versions of them, but she didn't have to think this story up. She just told it. She knew it, almost as if she had been there, as if she had entertained the Devil. Old Lady Mary treats the Devil as a casual guest, at the human level. More like a person than a spirit; at the end he admits that she knows more than he does.*

Mary Jones

19

Charles: *But in fact, she falls into his trap as he makes her do evil.*

Rose: *Perhaps, but that's not the way Old Lady Mary told it.*

Old Lady Mary and the Heifer Shoes

The Devil dashed up on Old Go Faster, that old horse of his and stopped at Old Lady Mary's house. After she had done told him to lite and look at his saddle, he pranced up the walk and sat down on the doorstep. He just sat there with his head in his hands. When Old Lady Mary up and asked him what he was worrying about, he told her that he was having trouble with Old Man Judson and his old woman. They just got along too good. Never had any arguments and never had any fights. Just couldn't get them into any sort of disturbance. Devil said he tried night and day to start a ruckus between that old man and woman; but they were just as loving and kind as husband and wife should be, and paid no attention to any of his capers.

Then Old Lady Mary laughed and laughed until she nearly 'bout fell down; and she told the Devil that she had more power than he did and could make them old folks fall out.

Devil then promised he was going to bring Old Lady Mary a pair of heifer shoes if she could stir up trouble between the old man and woman.

Devil left and Old Lady Mary set out for Old Man Judson's

house. Found his old woman putting a spider of bread in front of the fire; told her if she wanted to keep her old man in a good humor all the time to cut off some of his chin whiskers when he went to sleep, wrap the whiskers in a rag and wear 'em in her shoe. Call that having the old man under foot. Just walk on him all the time. The old woman laughed and said she surely would try what Old Lady Mary said.

Then Old Lady Mary racked off down to the field to see Old Man Judson. Told him that his old woman was going to cut his throat the next time he went to sleep. Done heard her say so. Better watch what she was going to do. Old man said he was going to keep his eyes open, and thanky ma'am.

And that night after he went to bed, his old woman fixed to cut off some of the old man's whiskers. He jumped up and pretty near killed that old woman with a chair. They fought and fought and then they fought some more.

Next day the Devil rode up on Ole Over Comer, that other old horse of his, and threw the pair of heifer shoes on Old Lady Mary's doorstep. He was scared to go near that old woman since she was a whole lot smarter than he was.

And Old Judson and his old woman have been fighting from that day to this.

Charles: *Why didn't you check some of this folklore for sources at the university library?*

Rose: *I just didn't think about it. In fact, these stories were so peculiar in themselves I would not have thought of looking. I did read some, but it took a lot away from it too, the Uncle*

Judson Jones

Remus stories. I felt like that was older than the word, the little foxes and the rabbits.

Charles: *Took away some of the magical quality?*

Rose: *That's what I thought.*

Charles: *But at the time you felt like that you were in touch with professional folklorists like Howard Odum.*

Rose: *Yes, I was. I don't know why I didn't. I was just enjoying it.*

Charles: *Why publish?*

Rose: *Because I thought the old blacks should be heard from, their culture, and that there probably never would be any more stories like these, not exactly.*

Charles: *Is there anything else that you can tell me about Mary Jones?*

Rose: *Nothing except that she was a laughing, frolicking, jolly old lady. Her husband was old Judson, who farmed. He sat down and laughed when she told the story as though he was in on the joke too.*

Charles: *So he was audience to a story he had heard often?*

Rose: *Yes. I think they liked to tell and listen both. They swapped stories. It was because at that time they didn't have as much to amuse them as they do now. Plus, the art of storytelling. I felt it, more than I know, because I have been to see some lately and their minds were cluttered.*

Rose and I had taken a new tape recorder out one afternoon to try some interviewing. We sat on a black friend's porch and she talked a great deal about nothing and kept stopping to wave and exchange greetings with an unusually large number of passersby for such a remote setting, or so it seemed to us.

Rose: *In telling a story like "The Heifer Shoes," they were not thinking about a whole lot of other things.*

Charles: *Have radio and television cluttered their minds, the few you have tried to interview recently?*

Rose: *Well, that could have been some of it and then changes that have come in the way of life, the things that happen all around them. Sally, for example, distracted by passersby.*

Much of Greene County is red clay but the part of it in and around White Plains is gray sandy loam, thus the title "That Grayland Road." There is actually no one road so named, although the two women who told Rose the story seem to have a particular one in mind. Even though the women talk of the characters in the story as if they were part of the community, they do not indicate whether they knew them personally or genuinely believed the story.

Rose: *The names of the two women standing there (in the photograph) are Annie Mae Armor and Corine Berry. This was way back in the 1930s. I had already heard the story but had not gotten it down. I remembered it one day when I was passing a field where two women were chopping cotton, nearby what was supposed to be "that Grayland Road." I stopped and asked them if they ever walked the old Grayland Road. They stopped work, thought, and said, "We used to walk that Grayland Road but not since ole Cahline Bray and Emeline Shaw walked it that night. It was a white rabbit."*

24

Annie Mae Armor and Corine Berry

That Grayland Road

Well, yes, we walked it—that Grayland road. But not since old Cahline and not since old Emeline traveled it one night. They were coming from meeting or might have been going to that little chapel over there. Yes, Sis Cahline and, oh well, yes, Sis Emeline were coming or maybe they were going—when a little old white rabbit crossed in front of them, and squatted right there beside the road. They never even heard him, but Lawsy, yes, they saw him in the bright moon-shiny night.

Now, that old Cahline, she kept on going for she knew the creature wasn't natural when she saw him squatting there. But, old Emeline was a curious old woman and she stayed 'til she saw what it was. And that rabbit, he surely beat her; yes, beat her and killed her dead. He killed Sis Emeline in the middle of that Grayland Road.

Now, none of the folks will walk it—never even go along that way. But Sis Emeline, I tell you, is never off it. She is all the time just traveling that scary old road.

Rose: *I asked what happened to Cahline. They said that folks just forgot about her. I asked why then did they remember Emeline. At first they hesitated to answer. Then they said, "Cause she's still walking that Grayland Road." Annie Mae and Corine both wanted to tell the story and they alternated telling the details and getting them straight. Kind of a duet: "Yes, Sis Cahline," and the other, "Yes, Sis Emeline." One's "Walk that Grayland Road" rhythmically answered by the other's "Yes, that Grayland Road." They said that folks said that Sis Emeline was never off "that Grayland Road."*

Charles: *Were they consciously giving a folk notion a local habitation and a name?*

Rose: *It's hard to say. A good storyteller will do that, you know. The old man who told me "Cats Toting a Cat" said he didn't believe all of that story.*

Charles: *Speaking of cats, tell me about "Liddy Purify's Cat." First, I don't believe anybody was named "Purify."*

Rose: *That was the old negro's version of the family name*

Purefoy. *Dora Lawson of Greene County told this one. She was Aunt Pat's nurse. Liddy Purify lived down this way not far from my house. Dora was an exaggerator; she wanted to make a good story out of whatever she told. Liddy Purify had this old cat and one day when they were sitting around in the yard, a chicken hawk picked up the cat and took it high into the air.*

Liddy Purify's Cat

I was right there on the doorsteps with Aunt Liddy Purify when that chicken hawk caught her poor little cat. He was under a tree with his eyes half shut, that little old cat was.

Liddy Purify's House

Liddy Purify

Never has been worth much anyway so everybody says. That hawk just swooped down and grabbed that little old cat and went straight up with him and sailed pretty near out of sight. Liddy Purify said there goes my poor little cat. And about that time, it started to get dark—and it was broad open daylight. It looked mighty strange and we didn't know what to do. But about that time we saw the feathers just a dropping down—you just naturally couldn't see the sun for them. Then we saw that old chicken hawk and that pitiful cat come circling down—after a while they lit in the spot where they rose from. That chicken hawk had lost all his feathers except a few on his wings. That cat had just about picked him clean. The old hawk looked right shamefaced and he dropped the cat and sidled on off. The cat didn't do a thing but sit down under the same tree and shut his eyes like he was half asleep.

Liddy Purify said that cat was naturally no good anyhow.

Charles: *What do you think really happened that Dora is embroidering on?*

Rose: *Well, I think the hawk did catch the cat and might have gone a little ways with him, but I don't think it lost a single feather. It's pure exaggeration. It would have been a sorry story if something had not happened up in the air. Dora knew that, so she just let the cat pick him clean.*

I Was a Mighty Dancer

Rose: *Dora, who told me about Liddy Purify's cat, had a good sense of humor. She knew everybody, it seemed. She exaggerated a lot about those people at Mr. John's place.*

Charles: *Tell me about that story, but first let's get the names straight: Miss Pat, who is also called Aunt Sis, is your father's sister?*

Rose: *Yes, those are the two names we called her.*

Charles: *She was Patricia Thompson?*

Rose: *No, she was Martha Elizabeth Thompson, my aunt. When my mother first got sick and we children would be worried, we'd say, "Aunt Sis, is Mother real sick?" "Oh no, child, she's not so sick" or "You come on in here and help me string these beans." She'd give you something to do, but you felt just as safe if she told you; the doctor couldn't have made me feel any better. She was the one who told me all the stories, things that happened. There was one story, charming to a child for its repetition. It was "Pick, Child, Pick."*

Once there was a little girl who went along to church and sat behind a very rich lady with jewels all over her dress. Well, this little girl began picking the jewels off. The rich lady turned around and said, "Pick, child, pick." And then she

Dora Lawson

would turn the other way and she would say, "I wish you would make your little girl stop picking the jewels off my dress." The mama would do something to the little girl to stop her, I guess, but the little girl would start picking the jewels again and the rich lady would say to her, "Pick, child, pick. The more you pick, the more you'll have." And that is all I can remember, just the repetition of that phrase.

Charles: *She just made it up?*

Rose: *I don't know where she got all those stories. She'd tell stories about animals and people. About the animals: one time the old owl said to the fox, "Fox, I got some pretty babies; please don't bother them." He said, "Suppose you tell me what they look like so I won't bother them." She said, "They are the prettiest ones in the forest." Well, when he got to the owls, he thought they were the ugliest in the forest and ate them up.*

If you wanted to go hunting nuts, there were some trees way over in the woods called scaley-bark trees, sort of a hickory nut. They were very good to eat. We would all want to go, and mother would say, "You can't go by yourself."

Charles: *Was that from this White Plains house?*

Rose: *No, that was when we lived near Liberty Church. So, we would go and say, "Aunt Sis, would you go scaley-bark hunting with us?" She would say, "Of course, I will; get you some bags to put your nuts in." She would go clear across the creek with us. She would go 'possum hunting with the older ones, but I was too young to get in on those. She was a sport. She was a maiden lady. She used to be a schoolteacher and she had gone to a boarding school. She stayed with her father and kept house for him. That was William Floyd Thompson. She didn't demand anything of us. I never heard her wanting anything.*

Charles: *Is all of this by way of telling me about Dora's story of Mr. John's place?*

Rose: *Yes. As she got older she became an invalid. At the time of Dora's telling me the story, she was living in a little house in Mary Will's yard.*

Charles: *Mary Will is her niece, Mrs. Carl Thompson?*

Rose: *Yes. A regular little house, a kitchen and everything. And Mary Will said that those years with Miss Pat were some of the happiest of her life, because she learned so much from Miss Pat. Aunt Sis was very intelligent. She did not read a lot then, but she knew people. I don't really know what she had, but what she had was wonderful, something special. That afternoon I went up there, Dora Lawson was her nurse, and Dora had worked as a house maid, an errand girl, they called them, on Mr. John's place when she was a young girl. Aunt Sis had known all of these same people too. When I came into the room, they were talking about some of the people who had worked at Mr. John's place. She was a very lively invalid and she seemed to be in charge of the discussion. When she saw me, she said, "We might as well start over. Rose will want to hear about the old times too." Dora turned to me and asked, "You want to hear about the folks who used to work at Mr. John's place?" Then she started to tell about each one.*

Old Man John's Place

You want to hear about all the folks that used to live at Old Man John's place? I have got so old and painful that I have nearly forgot those old folks. Where are they now? Well some of them have gone one way and some another. Where is Old Rilla Roach? I don't know where the Lord saw fit to send Old Aunt Rilla. She has been dead going on more than three years.

What did all of us do at Old Man John's place? Bless your time, some were doing one thing and some of us were doing another; but everybody was powerful busy. Old Miss was all the time walking around with her little old key basket right on her arm, seeing if things were going right in the house. Old Man John kept everything going right in the yard. Lawsy me, Old Man John got about so fast that his misbehavior coat stood straight in the wind most of the time. A misbehavior coat was nothing but just a frocktail coat that slapped you when you walked.

Yes, everybody had a job to do at that place. There was Old Man Fate that saw about everything around the place. He saw after the saddle horses and he raised a son for a carriage boy. He said that he could do anything that mortal man could do, and it seemed that it was the truth. That old man was a caution.

Old Sugar Bill? Lawdee, I haven't seen that old man in a coon's age. Why did they call him Sugar Bill? Well, when he was a little boy, he used to stay around the house and help Old Miss. He was the cowboy that drove up the cows in the evening and brought in chips to start a fire with the next morning. He was the favorite of the little black children, and called himself helping Old Miss when she baked tea cakes. If she didn't watch him mighty close he would get into the sugar keg. He loved sugar so powerful good that Old Miss took to calling him Sugar Bill.

Yes'm, Grandma Abbey was most too old to work around the yard but she surely was a nice old lady, and nice 'til she died. She used to be a mighty seamster; used to go out and

36

look at the lilies of the fields and then make quilts just like them. And there was Old Aunt Lucy Harris, who didn't do a thing but make wine. Then she poured it into demijohns and Old Miss would take it up to the wine room and let it stay about fifty years.

What is that you say? Old Aunt Sleepy Mariah never did do anything but sit on the side of the road and sleep. And while she was asleep folks would go by and take everything the poor creature had. Then she would wake up long enough to go to church and then go right back to sleep again. Folks said that her mother gave her a markment because she used to sit and watch the hogs sleep all of the time.

No, that's not all the folks that worked at the old place. There was old Aunt Nicey that cooked at the big house and then there was Kizzie that cooked for the field workers. Old Miss used to go to and fro from one of those kitchens to the other. She would come tipping in with white knit gloves on and then rub her hand on the table to see if there was a speck of dirt anywhere. Old Miss was a sight in this world. We called her Miss Blackie Top because she used to wear a black hat and veil when she went visiting. She used to ride a big old horse named Flora that was a pacer; and Brown Rabun, the carriage boy, used to hang on to old Flora's tail so he would be there to hitch the horse for Old Miss. Folks said the reason that Brown was always short of breath was because he was always trying to keep up with that old horse.

That was a real saddle that Old Miss rode on. You could hear it crying about a mile off. Well, Old Nicey used to sit in the kitchen door and listen, and when she heard that old saddle crying she knew it was time to put the biscuit on to cook. She would say she heard Old Miss and Brown Rabun coming home; then she would say, "This not doing me, let me get up from here and get dinner on."

Yes'm, I'll tell you about the others that worked there; but I have got like a grandfather clock—I take my time. There was Sooky, Narcissy, and another old woman named Octavia that helped around the yard, besides all the field workers. I surely remember Aunt Hetty. She used to be a mighty hand to shout—had a praying ground in the corner of the fence where she used to go to pray and shout. The year that the Lord came along with the big storm, everybody begged old Hetty to start a-praying.

Nobody could forget old man Hilliard. He used to buttle* around the house and he always butchered the cows. He was a little old hairy-faced curious-looking man and went half bent all the time; but then he wasn't as strange looking as old Louis Cannon. Louis was the cowherd and stayed out in the pasture and salted the cows. Used to hear him all the time calling the cows; and when they heard him calling, "Coo, sheep," they sure enough put their feet to the ground. Old Louis wore his hair long and plaited like a woman's, and they say he stayed with the cows so much that he acted like one. Then when he died folks said that cows came for him. But I am not a hand to speak against the dead because I am going to be called into death some of these days.

The next time you pass Old Man John's place, you may see an old woman sitting beside the road. They say that Old

*served as butler

39

In the Peach Orchard

Missouri stays there all of the time; she thinks all of the old folks are still there—and says that her granddaddy and grandmammy are still scouting around there because that was their plantation. She says that she is about six hundred years old and that she is Methuzler's sister.

I am not what I once was but Old Dora still has the desire,

and I still turn my hands to what I can. Yet and still, my longest days are past.

Rose: *But Aunt Sis was not satisfied with Dora's telling and would frequently correct her. When Dora said that she didn't know what the Lord had seen fit to do with Rilla Roach, Aunt Sis said, "It's none of your business anyway, Dora." When Dora claimed that Grandma Abbey could look at the lilies of the field and make quilts just like them, Aunt Sis said, "I have given Grandma Abbey many a quilt pattern, and they were not lilies of the field." Aunt Sis didn't believe that Old Aunt Lucy Harris or anybody else would keep a good wine for fifty years. When Dora said that Old Miss went from one kitchen to the other, Aunt Sis said, "That's about all she ever did. I never heard of her working." When Dora said that Ole Miss used to ride a horse named Flora, Aunt Sis said that that was not so, that her horse was named Flora, and that whenever she and Flora crossed a creek, Aunt Sis would say, "Surely goodness and mercy will follow me all the days of my life."*
Charles: *Why did she quote the psalm?*
Rose: *To thank God for getting safely across. It was a high creek; horse had to swim some. Aunt Sis took strong exception to Dora's suggesting that the carriage-boy Brown Rabun used to hang onto the tail of Ole Miss's Flora so that he could be there to help her alight. "The very idea," she humphed, "another one of Dora's tales." When Dora was through, Aunt Sis's final summation: "Too much talk went on at that old place anyhow."*

41

Charles: *Did you ever identify Mr. John's last name and the location of his place?*

Rose: *His place was where Putnam, Greene, and Hancock counties come together. I'm not sure which county it actually lay in.*

Charles: *What was his last name?*

Rose: *I didn't get that; just the story.*

Charles: *How did Dora take all of those interruptions?*

Rose: *She was amused. They were good buddies and liked to argue a bit. It passed the time. They knew each other's ways. Aunt Sis had an iron named Old Betsy. It was about three inches tall and maybe eight inches long, with a handle. You could take the top off and fill it with hot charcoals. Aunt Sis would iron a lot of clothes with Old Betsy. We talked about Betsy like she was a person. About ten years ago, we said, "Whatever happened to Old Betsy?" We started looking for her but never did find her. Anything Aunt Sis did had an originality to it.*

Rose: *I got this story near Milledgeville in Baldwin County, Georgia. A little seven-year-old girl named Sue Ella Lane told me this story. I had gone to see her grandfather, Fred Sanders, but he wasn't there. Only some of the children were in the yard of this small tenant house. Sue Ella was the smallest of them, and when I started making conversation about tales to tell, she jumped up and told this one without prompting or interruption. She had a lot of spontaneity. They lived on the old Carrington place.*

Grandma's Ground Pea Patch

One time there was a little boy going down the road sing-ing a little lonesome song that sounded sort of pitiful like this.

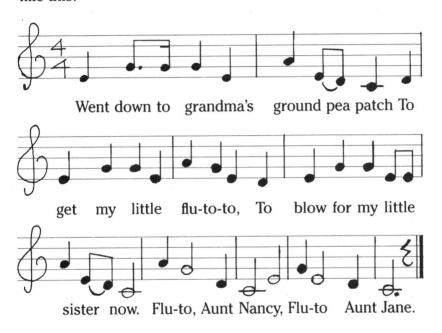

Went down to grandma's ground pea patch To

get my little flu-to-to, To blow for my little

sister now. Flu-to, Aunt Nancy, Flu-to Aunt Jane.

Then he went on down the road 'til he met a little fox. The fox said, "Boy! Where are you going?"
"Been down to Grandma's ground pea patch," the little boy said.
"For what?" asked the fox.

"To get my little flu-to-to," said the little boy.

Then the fox said, "What did you fetch it for?"

And the little boy said right pitiful, "To blow for my little sister, now, flu-to, Aunt Nancy, flu-to Aunt Jane."

"Can you sing it?" asked the little old fox.

"Yes sir," said the boy.

"Let me hear you then," said the fox. And he set down on his haunches and shut his eyes, because he liked to hear music.

Then the little boy sang that song a heap sadder than he had ever sung it before.

The fox said, "That's a powerful sad song." And then he racked on down through the woods blinking his eyes right fast.

The little boy started on down the road again and he met the Devil right in the bend of the road. The Devil stopped dead in his tracks, and he said, "Where have you been, boy?"

The little boy was so scared he could hardly talk but he knew he was obliged to be polite to the Devil so he said sort of pitiful, "Been down to Grandma's ground pea patch."

"For what?" asked the Devil.

And the little boy said, "For to get my little flu-to-to."

"For what?" said the Devil like he is getting out of patience with the little boy.

The boy was so scared that his legs gave away under him, but he said, "To blow for my little sister now, flu-to Aunt Nancy, flu-to Aunt Jane."

Then the little boy shut his eyes and hoped that the Devil would be gone when he opened his eyes again. But about

Sue Ella Lane

that time the Devil reached down and caught the poor little boy and crammed him into a sack and threw the sack over his back and hurried on home.

When he got there, he locked the little boy up in a room and left him right by himself. Then the Devil went off about his business.

After a while, the Devil's wife heard the little boy singing that sad little old song, and she cracked open the door and said, "What is that you are singing about, little boy?"

And he said, "I am singing about going to Grandma's ground pea patch."

"Let me hear you sing it then," the Devil's wife said.

And the little boy said, "I can sing it a heap better if you will open the door a little wider so I can get some air."

Then the Devil's wife opened the door a little wider and then the little boy sang the song.

Went down to Grandma's ground pea patch
To get my little flu-to-to,
To blow for my little sister now.
Flu-to, Aunt Nancy, flu-to Aunt Jane.

And Lord, bless my soul, that little boy sang that song so pitiful that the Devil's wife nearly about cried her eyes plumb out. She cried so hard that she didn't see the little boy when he slipped out through the crack in the door and went running down that road.

Rose: *Louisa Lattimer came by our house in White Plains one day, and we sat and talked. I gave her a cup of coffee,*

Louisa Lattimer

and she went in to speak to Mother, who was sick in bed by then. Louisa was an old lady whom I had known for a long time. She would chide you for something you didn't do right. And she got me that day.

Charles: *What had you done wrong?*

Rose: *I hadn't known Aunt Dilsey Brown. She had lived here in Greene County over near Pierce's Chapel. Louisa said with a scolding tone in her voice, "You didn't know Aunt Dilsey? Everybody knows Aunt Dilsey. She passed your house many a time. Everybody knows Aunt Dilsey." She made me feel that I had missed a great person by being the exception. And I had. This was in the early 1940s and Aunt Dilsey was dead by then. Louisa Lattimer was an old woman then too.*

Everybody Knew Aunt Dilsey

Don't you remember Old Aunt Dilsey? Why child, everybody knew Aunt Dilsey. She has passed your house many a time; a little old woman all dressed in black, and carrying a little old doctor-woman bag. Haven't you ever seen her? Folks would run to the window and say there goes Aunt Dilsey to catch another baby out of the river. She caught many a one to be sure. How old was she? Well, it didn't make any difference how old she was. She might have been ninety or she might have been more but that surely didn't bother Aunt Dilsey. She was a powerful frolicker. Haven't you ever seen her dance? She could dance with a glass of water on her head and never spill a drop; then do the cake walk, lean over backwards, touch her head to the floor, and lift one leg way up in the air.

Law, me—she came up the path on Christmas morning and after she had caught everybody Christmas gift, she said she was going to Santa Claus me. The way she cut up was enough. She set in and told old tales, danced the buzzard lope and rejoiced because it was Christmas.

Then she told the children how the sun was going to shout* on Christmas morning. Sure enough, the sun shouted just like Aunt Dilsey said it would. My goodness alive, do you mean to say you haven't ever seen the sun shout on Christmas morning?

---

*Just as the sun comes up on Christmas morning, long rays of sparkling light reach out in every direction from the sun.

There has never been anybody just like Aunt Dilsey. She was a straight up and down lady day and night. But, she surely was a powerful dancer; the only way she could keep from dancing when the children picked the box* was to get up and leave the room.

Yet and still, she could turn right around and explain the preacher's text faster than he could take it.

Law, child, everybody knew Aunt Dilsey.

But she sickened and died.

Rose: *Louisa Lattimer was perceptive herself.*

Charles:*And good at expressing what she saw. In just a few minutes she gave you a vivid portrait of Aunt Dilsey.*

Rose: *Yes. She was dramatic and kept to the point. You see, when she mentioned Aunt Dilsey, I asked just one question: Who is Aunt Dilsey? Then the whole sketch came out uninterrupted. Sometimes in collecting these stories it was my questions during pauses which brought forth the details, but not this time. Once Louisa had started her answer, she had no further need for me. When she left, I felt I was due to be scolded for not having known Aunt Dilsey.*

Charles: *You have been calling some of these blacks Uncle and Aunt even though those terms are no longer appreciated. Why do you?*

Rose:*Because it was a term of respect sincerely meant and so received. When my brother John was about five years old, a little black boy named Steve was his playmate and was also to look after him. Steve must have been about seven. My*

*guitar

49

Boys in the Farmyard

brother called him Steve, but Steve told him, "Don't you say that, boy. You say Uncle Steve, Uncle Steve!" So, like Steve, in the past I used those terms to show respect. Today I show respect to my black friends by not using those terms.

Rose had heard that Mama Lou still lived on a farm near White Plains. She had been the nurse-companion of Rose's father when he was a boy.

Rose: *I hadn't known the old woman before I went there, but I had known who she was. She had been my father's nurse when he was small, and she must not have been much older than he. At the time I went, my father was quite old and remembered when Mama Lou had been a little girl. And when I got to the house, she was polite, cordial enough, but she didn't really open up to me all of this until I told her that she had looked after my father. Then she asked, "Well, how is little Jimmy?" From then on it was easy, and we talked about things in general, and she wanted to talk about how he was getting along. Then she was not strong and well, but she was happy enough to have me there. I finally hit upon the idea of asking her if she had gone to dances when she was young, and she said, "Lord, I was a mighty dancer! Light on my feet, was I light!" And from then on she talked about how she felt about religion and then she would talk of dancing and the joy of it and the fun when they went to frolic and how she would look after Ole Miss the next day.*

Charles: *Was Ole Miss your mother or grandmother?*

Rose: *Neither. She was the woman Mama Lou worked for later.*

Charles: *Why did she mix the two subjects so?*

Rose: *Because she loved dancing and had been told that it was sinful. When she wanted to tell of the joy of dancing she kept weaving in repentance for it. At first I thought that I had nothing at all, just pieces of a story. Then I saw how unconsciously Mama Lou had woven the themes together. So I wrote it down in the same manner. Although she had been sanctified and had no place in her life for dancing and such, she still remembers it, calls and all.*

I Was a Mighty Dancer

Lord, yes, I was a mighty dancer! But I don't want to dance those old dances now—want to run from them. Want to get to heaven.

What did they play? Fiddles, that's what they played. Don't they have fiddles now?

Lord, dancing! I did love it—oh yes, and the banjos. Can't you hear the banjos?

But I have let that thing alone, and I am glad of it. Now I have been born of the Spirit; my Lord has turned me clean around.

What sort of figgers did they cut? Don't know child—I have plumb forgot. I'd have to get up and cut the pigeon wing and I can't cut anymore figgers. I have been sanctified!

Swing and change!
Promenade all!

I have forgot all about it. But, I was a mighty dancer—no need for me to tell a story about it. I was a dancer right.

And child, when I was out on the floor, all of the boys would ask me to dance.

Rustle your bustle, Miss Josephine.
Shake that thing, Darleen.

And when they looked at me, I saw that every one of them had a courting disposition and a marrying desire.

Was I light on my feet? You know I was, child—dance my way into the night.

That was the time we dressed up. Oh my—such a hopping

Mama Lou

about on the floor; dresses a waving around—fiddles tuning up.

Lady round the lady
And the gent don't go.

That was dancing! Wouldn't be tired when you stopped your feet from dancing—just had to stop so you could wait on Ole Miss next day. We called them frolics; boys would ask you to go to a frolic at such and such a place. Then you fixed up in your best bib and tucker and set out.

That we did.

Swing on the corners
and promenade all

But I've let such things alone, thank the Lord—have let those old things go by. They are not any good to me now.

How come it is a sin to dance? I don't know. But the Lord surely is not going to take you up to heaven while you are kicking up your heels and prancing around. You have got to live humble and go down on bended knee. Pray a while and then pray some more.

Yet and still, I was a mighty dancer. There were some who were light on their feet and could get about; and I surely could get over the floor.

But I am an old lady now. Don't see a place for me to frolic anymore. I laid that thing down to pick it up no more.

I am looking toward Zion and the river that never runs dry. Just the way I liked to dance, that's the way I love to pray. All those things have gone; and praise the Lord, I've been sanctified.

HALLELUJAH!
But yet and still—I was a mighty dancer.
>*Hop light ladies*
>*The cake's all dough*
>*Lady round the lady*
>*And the gent don't go.*

Charles: *About how old was she?*

Rose: *I would say that she was about ninety in 1945 when I saw her.*

Charles: *And that's the generation that you have interviewed that makes these people unique, at least the stories they told you. Tell me about their household.*

Rose: *I don't know all of them. But there was a granddaughter there visiting from Cleveland or Chicago, and she didn't quite understand what I wanted from her grandmother, or she didn't want to reveal all of her feelings to me. She was restless; she would walk all over the room and wouldn't have anything to say, but I could tell she was unhappy about it. If she had lived with her grandma, I think she would have understood, but she didn't like it too much. She was a young girl. She didn't realize that this was her own culture, the things that her grandmother was revealing to me.*

Sound
the Trumpet

Millie Simmons and her husband Robert were among Rose's best friends. She has three stories by Millie: "The Lord Sets High," "Ring the Charming Bells," and "Hy-Ty." Rose had over a period of time said so much in passing about Millie Simmons that I asked her to talk just about her.

Charles: *You said that Millie was lighthearted and fun-loving but that you learned the other side of Millie. Tell me about that side.*

Rose: *It came up one day when she said that she had been to the funeral of a friend. Then she told me about how "the Lord sets high."*

The Lord Sets High

The Lord sets high, yes, child—but then He looks low; and I am going to give you nothing but the truth out of my heart.

Religion just come in me when I was a child; always had

a spirit of do right in my soul—just borned in me—just borned in me.

Go to sleep at night and be traveling in a vision, sometime at a spring and a whole lot of little lambs come round and look in my face. Be at a spring dipping water—watering the sheeps.

Meant just what the Lord intended it to be. Lord meant me to save His sheep, feed His sheep. Told Peter to feed His sheep, told Peter to feed His lambs.

Now, I have done watered and fed them lambs—just like Peter, that old saint. Faithful!

In a wheat field: just a waving—the wheat. Little path no wider than nothing at all. Little sheep in the wheat field following me. And I was leading them. I was in the wheat field and I followed that little narrow path. The little sheeps right behind me, coming with me—and Christ done say lead my sheep.

Dropped off to sleep—angel met me; come on, been looking for you a long time. Follow me. Has a song want you to sing with me. Lawsy, can't sing with you; oh yes you can. Now, you sing this little song with me. Angel sing the song and I still carry it in my heart.

Carried me up the stairs—up and up and up—never did get to the end—singing as we went, up the stairs with the angels.

Angel make me a little crown and set it right up on my head. How are you able to make crowns like this, I asked. And when she done sing that song again, angel say such a few done climbed them stairs that they can give a crown to all that come.

Millie Simmons

Rose: *She said that she had had a vision which she would tell me about. I think it has elements of the Twenty-Third Psalm in it—especially through the valley of death and the still waters. Also, the "feed my sheep" passage. Perhaps, too, an echo of "feed my sheep, Peter" from John 21:15. To me she was a most unusual person. You could see that in her face, hear it in her voice. She was beautiful, bright of face and soul. It was a comforting face. You would want to go to see her when you were in trouble. Maybe that's the reason I saw her so much. So reassuring just to be with her.*

Charles: *How did you know that Millie had this religious side?*

Rose: *I started to tell you that when she told me that she had been to the funeral of a friend and that she knew her friend was in heaven right then, I asked her what was heaven like and that's when she told me about the charming bells.*

Ring the Charming Bells

Heaven is a happy and a holy place—and you're going to enjoy all the glories if you go there: see a rainbow about the throne, and all those golden streets. Everything glorious! And there are pearly gates—such a coming and going through the pearly gates. There's a keeper of the gates, some of those old patriarchs. But the gates, the pearly gates, won't be shut at all by day, and there—there is no night. It's always day, bright shiny day.

And the stars in heaven shine so bright, beautiful, beautiful silver light. Oh yes, stars in heaven. But that city has no need for the sun, nor the stars, nor the moon to brighten it. The glory of God shines all about. They rejoice and be happy in heaven. They sing and rejoice in that happy, holy place. And they ring those charming bells.

Got crowns of glory—starry crowns: and harps—they play on the harps; and the bells, charming bells for to ring.

You're going to meet the old Christians when you get to heaven. Don't know who they are but they will be there just marching the golden streets. The ones who are there now are marching those golden streets. And when you get in heaven, Old Father Moses will be looking out for you. Going to see Old Father Moses there watching out for you; and Old Father Gabriel is going to beckon you in. Oh yes there's glory in heaven, and you are going to ring the charming bells.

And there will be angels up there in white robes of righteousness; and crowns on their heads—starry crowns! Angels with harps in hands, flying all around. Yes, child, they got wings.

Yes, Lord, heaven's a high and righteous place, and the chariot is going to take you home.

When you get to heaven the journey has done end; and you're going to join in and ring the gloryful bells—you're going to ring the charming bells.

Rose: *Walking those golden streets sounded such a sameness but the way Aunt Millie told it, it was not tiresome, it was beautiful. After Millie told it, I could see those men. Isn't it strange that I thought of the men? All those old patriarchs marching along. "Charming Bells" came first; that's how I knew she had that deeper religious aspect. When I went home and transcribed my notes, I realized that she had said "chiming bells" but I so preferred the "charming bells" that I had misheard, that I left the error in.*

Charles: *Is there anything else about Millie?*

Rose: *Yes. The minute you met her you knew that you would like her and that you could trust her completely. I remember that sometimes I would see Millie and Robert on the street in Milledgeville, and it was such a pleasure to meet up with them. They lived on the Lower Macon Road and would bring eggs to sell. We would stop to chat, and Millie would say, "Look here, Robert, who done stopped to talk to us."*

I had first met Millie showing her how to use a pressure cooker. She had never had one. This young supervisor and I were sort of playing hooky one day. It was nearly Christmas and he was looking for a baby goat to give for a Christmas gift. We went to Millie and Robert's, hunting that goat when we should have been in the office. We felt welcome at their house.

Robert was a good farmer, substantial, although his hant stories make him sound a bit flippant. He was a tall man with a gray mustache and a twinkle in his eye. Millie might have been the leader, in a way, in that family; never a note of discord, I'm sure.

I don't know what led up to Hy-Ty, but Robert seems to have originated him and Millie and others contributed details as

63

the story got retold. They almost accept Hy-Ty as a reality. Robert seemed to be the expert on him, although it was Millie who told much of the story. They told it together, alternately adding to or correcting the other. Robert started by saying that the last time he had seen old High Tower, Hy-Ty was sitting a-straddle of the gin house. I think that Millie said that folks out there all knew the story although they might not know that there was no such things as a hant, that the story just stayed with them.

Old Hy-Ty

There was an old hant who used to travel the road all the time. He was so tall—nearly about as tall as a tower, that they took to calling him Hy-Ty. One time some folks killed a man and put him back on his horse and he's been traveling ever since. That is old Hy-Ty. Once a man climbed a tree so he could scare the womanfolks when they passed along on their way to church. But whilst the man was up the tree, old Hy-Ty come prancing down the road; and his head reached way up in the tree where the man was. Scared the man so bad that he turned loose and dropped right down in the road. Broke nearly every rib he had.

Old Hy-Ty was a sight back in the old days but you don't see him on the road much now; reckon he is scared he will get run over with his old long self. Last time I saw that old

65

Robert Simmons

hant, he was setting right a-straddle of the gin house—with one foot on one side and one on the other side.

But, law me, the times have done changed; looks like there's not many old timey hants left. There was one night that we passed a whole regiment of hants right in the road. We felt the wind of them critters passing us. Nearly took my breath away as they flounced by.

There are hants just like there is everything else. Nobody knows where they come from or where they call themselves going. But one thing everybody knows, if you die and don't die happy, you are going to be on the road. And another thing, if you meet a hant he is going to let you know what he is.

Used to be one old hant that would swing overhead on a silver ladder. You could see him any night swinging backwards and forward. Didn't mean to harm anybody—just some poor soul gone to rest.

There was an old man who was always worrying about hants, and he talked about them enough. Well bless your time, once he was going on home and met a hant that had one arm and three fingers. That old hant nearly slapped that man's head off, and that proves you had better not meddle with a hant.

Rose: *Maybe Robert didn't create him. They didn't exactly believe in Hy-Ty, but with a good imagination and with hant stories that had been handed down to them, it was not too difficult to build up such a personality as Hy-Ty. When I go by there, I still look for old Hy-Ty, but Robert said that since there*

Grinding Cane

are so many cars now, ole Hy-Ty don't get out on the road so 'much. I don't believe in him, but he is a vivid personality to me.

Charles: *Did the young supervisor help Robert?*

Rose: *Yes, the Farm Security Administration helped Robert get better equipment, could for example show him how to plow with a different blade new to him. The supervisor was especially good with the older farmers. If a man was in the field plowing and the supervisor wanted to show him something different, he would first take the plow and plow a few rounds. The farmer liked that. It showed that this young man that they thought of as a boy could tell them some things because he could get out and do it himself.*

Robert was part of the farm program. The farm supervisor and the home supervisor would make out budgets and figure how much tenants like Robert and Millie would produce, for use or sale, and how much they would need for the next year.

It seemed to work pretty well although I never fully trusted those budgets—it was an estimate really. It would embarrass them because you would have to ask such personal questions. "How many shirts have you?" Maybe he didn't have but one or two. We would arrange grants-in-aid and help back up loans.

The Simmonses were reliable; they did their very best. There was something about them that made you feel better after you had visited them. I just liked to look at Millie. Her face was inspiring: you could almost see into her soul.

Charles: *Rose, we now move to some graver stories, first sad and then spiritually happy.*

Rose: *Yes, the beautifully sad one is "City Setting on a Hill." Mary Ann Jones of Baldwin County gave me that insight into a moment of her grief. That was in 1939; she was a Farm Security Administration client of mine. She was about fifty-five or so then. Her husband was Frank, a sharecropper. They lived on the road between Milledgeville and Sparta, back off the road. It was called McCombs Mount. The McCombs had owned the place. There was an old house back up there. The land was a little mountain, a rising.*

I remember sitting on Mary Ann's back-porch steps late in the afternoon, and I could see the lights of Milledgeville coming on, way down there in a valley it looked like, because we were so high. I had gone to take her some more recipes. But we had finished our talk about her garden, the chickens and things like that. Then we sat down on the steps to rest a little, and that was when she told me that she had a sorrow.

I had known her daughter a little when she was there at home. She was a very bright young girl. Some way she had been sent off to college, had a scholarship. Mary Ann was so proud of her. She was doing well but something had happened; Mary Ann never said what. But the way she expressed it: "My child done errored on the way."

As she talked, I realized that she was no longer talking to me: her words had become a prayer and I was humbled at being privileged to hear her lone talk with God.

City Setting on a Hill

I say,

Now, Lord I've seen a hard time in this world, and now I have another burden to bear—my child has errored on the way.

Lord, Lord, what am I going to do?

All of my days I have traveled the righteous roads, and always I have tried to be a city setting on a hill.

But now, Lord, I am heavy with trouble.

From the early light I bend over my work, but the tears on my face make my hands fumble at their task. Blessed Jesus, against all that I know the Lord has promised me a raiment to wear, and a place midst the heavenly throng.

Yes, Lord, my raising has brought me to where I am now, and I am going to carry it to the judgment bar; am not going to let my flag drag in the dust.

But, Lord, Lord, I bow my head.

For yet and still, my child has errored on the way.

Rose: *Frank was not there that afternoon. He was a good man. They were an unusual couple for their industry and thrift. He was a good sharecropper. He knew what good farming was; but he could not afford the equipment until FSA came along. Only the one child. Although I saw Mary Ann frequently after that, she never mentioned her daughter.*

Charles: *You weren't curious enough to ask?*

Rose: *That would not have been proper for me to bring the matter up. She was a very private person. She had given me a glimpse of what perhaps I shouldn't have seen. I just happened to have been there at the time.*

Charles: *I have been reading N. B. Puckett's* Folk Beliefs of the Southern Negro, *partly because it was published in 1926 and might give some information on the blacks of the age and time of your stories. He says that most of the blacks sold into slavery came from West Africa, where polytheistic religion abounded. He writes that although many of those natives believed in a Great God, he was ignored in favor of many particular gods with specialized powers to be propitiated, not loved. He writes, "The West African has nothing analogous to our Christ, a God-man connecting man with the great over-God, and this idea appeals to him when presented by Christianity, or Islam." He suggests, therefore, that a polytheistic heritage could account for the superstitions and beliefs in hants by black Christians. Does that ring true to you?*

Rose: *There could be some basis for that. They certainly have many beliefs handed down, just as in other cultures. An old woman in Greene County told me that she would be going*

Mary Ann Jones

home, and there would be a light in her window, and when she got there, there was no light. She was sure it was a hant. They believed in a spirit world.

Charles: *Yes, but don't others who do not have this West African background?*

Rose: *True. They had this hant tradition handed down from somewhere, perhaps Africa. At least blacks seemed to believe*

Pearl Armstrong

in hants and the like more openly, and maybe more generally, than the whites.

Charles: *Here's another Puckett idea: sin, defined as an offense against a deity, is not moral in West African religion but consists of an insult to the god or simply ignoring him. Do you find this at all applicable to the blacks whom you interviewed? Any division between morality and piety?*

Rose: *I have always thought that they might commit a lot of sins, but their religion was right there with them all the time. They believed.*

Charles: *Isn't that true of other people too?*

Rose: *How about David? He sinned but he could always pray. And the black Christian with his immediate faith could turn so quickly from sin to prayer.*

Charles: *Without complicated theology is your point?*

Rose: *That's it. He does not have to rationalize it: just like going from one room into another room. It's not a smaller moral sense; it's a bigger faith. It is just as natural as Pearl Armstrong's idea of good and evil. She was Aunt Sis's nurse. She told me about the two spirits.*

The Two Spirits

A person when he die has got two spirits—one spirit follows him wheresomever he goes and stops on the earth and stays such a length of time and then goes away on the wind. Spirits just have to go away—didn't everybody could see them and the whole world would be thick with nothing but spirits.

Two spirits surely follow you; and if you don't believe it, just go out on a moonshiny night and you will see two shadows. That's the two spirits—one the good and the other the evil spirit.

Whensomever the good spirit is with you, he drives that evil one out. The good spirit is the keeper of the house. Yes, there are two spirits—and God put them there, and nothing can we do about that. Don't know where they finally go for the dead ain't never told me what they do. You can see the two shadows anytime you take notice of them. The evil spirit goes along first, because most of the folks had rather follow the evil spirit.

Yes, Lord, the good spirit finally goes to God who gave it; and the evil spirit roams about in this old sinful world. Yes, the evil spirit stays on the earth such a length of time and then goes away on the wind.

But, let not your heart be heavy with trouble—for God's Spirit is here till the latter end.

Charles: *In the late nineteenth century, blacks "shouted" at church or in "praise-houses," shuffled in a ring in a quiet dance with some singing. Is that still what* shouting *means in the early and mid-twentieth century?*

Rose: *Not so much. It is singing, improvisational hymning, stately or highly emotional, sometimes with crying from possession of the Spirit. I remember once Becky Jane was singing, "shouting" to some ragtime records on an old phonograph instead of hymns, and someone said, "Becky Jane, don't you*

Sudie Harper

know you're shouting to that old ragtime?" Her answer: "I don't care; I'm going to take it all in!" You have got to remember their rich zest for life, their experiencing quality. They did not exclude as much, maybe. Religion was just a part. Like Emma: she was sitting with her new crochet hook and thread when her sister said, "Come on, Emma, it's time to go to church." Emma said, "I done got my religion and I just have learned how to do this."

Charles: *How about Sudie Harper?*

Rose: *I met Sudie Harper in 1939. She lived close to Eatonton. She helped me get the group together for a demonstration meeting for cooking, cheese making, or mattress making.*

Aunt Sudie was sort of leader in her community and a pillar in her church. I knew her daughter-in-law too. Sudie's husband was a sharecropper. When we were working, she would chat idly and quip. One day I said, "Well, Aunt Sudie, looks like everyone's having a baby this year." "Yes," she said, "but it's leap year, remember." But then in quieter moments we would talk and she would reveal her deep spiritual nature. On one occasion I got her idea of how prayer is immediate and is the key to glory.

Key to Glory

Without the Spirit nobody can pray: and whatsomever the revelations gives you, they are the things for you to speak. And that's a fearful thing! Do you hear it? The plan of salvation is so clean, and the Spirit does dwell in a sinful body. It's a clean way and I'm telling you just like it is: there surely is two of us. There's a natural one and a spiritual one, and the Good Spirit is the one that receives the substance of the Lord.

Something is going to pass over you when you pray—a fear. You can't go into the works of the Lord in any sort of way. There is nothing in it when you fail to obey the Lord but sorrow and trouble.

But, child, prayer is the key from this earth to glory!

And God is the Beginning, the Ending, the Author and the Finisher of all things.

Charles: *Did you find that most of the older blacks of that period had this deep religious sense?*

Rose: *Yes, more did than didn't. That deep belief that heaven is right up there and immediate. And that prayer brought God right here. I remember one day I was at Sol Napier's house. We were having a group meeting. A storm came up so bad that we couldn't see; we just quit what we were doing and huddled there. One person said, "If the Lord takes Carl today, He sure will get a Christian." I felt so safe there with them. I asked one of the children there whether he was afraid. He said simply, "No, Mama's praying." You can also see that secure certainty in Missouri Davenport's account of a total eclipse of the sun.*

Greene County Family

Dark Day

Have you ever heard of a Dark Day? I have seen one and that was sad—that was sad.

I was in the field
And I had my hoe,
I stood up
And folded my arms.

I said, "Well, Lord, I have always heard of the Judgment Day, and I am ready to hover my brood just like a hen hovers her chickens." Because when a child is twelve years old, the sins are on them; but all my children were little ones, and all their sins were on me. I haven't got one of the age.

I said, "Yes, Lord, all of us were on the way together." If our time was out, all of us were on the way together. All of us were going to cross the river of Jordan on the ship of Zion. I just stood there and folded my arms and looked for anything that might come. Lord, yes, I have heard about the Dark Day and been qualified to go. Yes, Lord, I have prayed. All the folks said there wasn't going to be a Dark Day. They said that God hadn't told anybody that the Dark Day was coming.

God hadn't even notified the angels in heaven, and that proved that man didn't know about it down here. They said that Dark Day wasn't going to be. But when that Dark Day did come, they all ran, they all cried out, "It's the Judgment, it's the Judgment!"

But, Lord, I just stood there and folded my arms. For I had been packing up for it—for the Judgment. I knew I didn't come here to stay; the rich and the poor, the old and the young—all of us come to go. Just like a peach gets ripe and falls off the tree. You have got to move when your time comes.

Lord, yes, honey, I saw that Dark Day,
        I was in the field
        And I had my hoe,
        I just stood there
        And folded my arms.
For I have prayed—and yes, Lord, I was qualified to go.

Rose: *Missouri lived in Baldwin County. As I sat with her one day while she was ironing her clothes, she told me about that day, her voice rising and falling to the rhythm of her ironing. In the midst of all that terror and confusion she seemed to have stood, unmoved, in the field, resolute and ready. I think I got more because I had been there a long time, visiting. It was such a pleasant place to be; I was relaxed myself. If I had gone in hurriedly and said I want a story from you, tell me something. . . . You had to go at it slowly, just like they did. You had to be a good listener and listen to every word, no eyes wandering. Anybody can tell when you don't give him your total attention. As I remember that day I sat and talked and didn't try to stop her from ironing, because I knew she needed to iron. I enjoyed the rhythm of her iron and voice. It was sort of musical to me. When I asked her whether she knew any stories from the old times, she said, well, she knew about the Dark Day. I didn't then ask her, "What are you going to tell me about the Dark Day?" I just sat there*

79

and listened. You had to be calm and relaxed like you were enjoying it, to make them feel easy. That was very easy for me, since I was so much enjoying it. And I didn't say, "Now, stop your work so you can tell me that story." She ironed right on and it blended in with her words. It was poetry to me.

Charles: *You wrote it down as poetry.*

Rose: *Yes, I like it that way.*

Charles: *Did she say this exactly? Did you polish it?*

Rose: *She said it and I didn't say anything. I knew that in her mind she was back in the field chopping cotton. I think I set it in that form so it would gain significance. That same abiding faith can be seen in "Us All Got to Go." I found it so lyrical that it seemed best to set it up as verse.*

Us All Got to Go

All of us got to go.
Yes, Lord, death is sure.
And you got to move when your time comes.
But when you trusts in God
He guides and watches over you
While you sleeps.
Sends the angels to witness and
Watch over you
While you sleeps—till morning
Light appears.
Us all got to trust in Him;

And when the Shepherd come in
He will lead you, and he will
Guide you.
Ain't going to lead you in no evil pathway—
Going to guide and protect you
In every sorrowing hour.
Yes, Lord, he's going to lead you
All the way in the paths of righteousness.
And if you was on the border of dying
The Good Shepherd would lead you,
Guide you,
Through the shadowy valley of death.
But all us come to go
Yes, Lord, death is sure.
And you got to move when your time come.
But, child, you mustn't be uneasy.
You needn't fear the wolf.
Nor another sort of evil.
You mustn't be 'shamed.
And when you come to die,
Let it be a soldier that go.

Charles: *Do you remember when you got that?*
Rose: *No, but I think it was from my friend Millie Simmons,
whom we already talked about. That belief that the spiritual
is immediate, is here, shows up in "Band of Angels." Minerva
Parham told me about her neighbor, who had recently had
a brush with angels. She said that that good old woman had*

Picking Cotton

always wanted to see an angel before she died because she thought that they were all around us all the time. Then Minerva told me about the band of singing angels.

Band of Angels

Old woman heard a band of angels singing up in the elements. The old woman did whilst she was a working in the garden. And she stopped and listened, and she looked up to the heavens. Eyes couldn't see the angels, but she surely heard them. Song they were singing, she just couldn't catch. But she heard a band of angels sing!

Charles: *Who was her friend?*

Rose: *It was Lillian Napier, who lived close to Minerva in Baldwin County. It was to Lillian's house that I went that time the storm came up. We were having a pressure-cooker demonstration. Sol Napier was her husband. They came from the old Napier place down in Baldwin. Lillian didn't see the angels, but she heard the music.*

Charles: *That same assured acceptance of other levels of being is in "Cows, They Pray" too, isn't it.*

Rose: *Yes. Bob Watkins told me that. Remember Uncle Robert, who laid fires of white wood on Sundays out of respect for the day? I told you that I always thought Uncle Bob could see more than most folks. He knew the cows were praying.*

Cows, They Pray

'Bout midnight they get down on their knees: Cows do— just a moaning, um, um, um-m.

Lord, yes, cows go to prayer. They pray all the time just like folks.

Saw a whole drove of cows in a ring, and they all went down together upon their knees. And all prayed: just amoaning um, um, um-m-m.

Cows go to prayer all the time—all times of night they at it.

Never heard of other critters pray; but cows does. Cows, they pray.

Charles: *Thomas Hardy has a lovely poem "The Oxen" in which a modern speaker remembers the tradition that oxen kneel on Christmas Eve and says that he did not doubt it or go check in earlier days and now he would be glad to go to the barn "in the gloom, Hoping it might be so."*

To change the subject a bit, I was quite honored once to be asked to speak the word at a funeral. Would you explain that tradition?

Rose: *For the funeral of a very good person the preacher would arrange in advance for people who wanted to give a testimonial for the deceased. That speech is called "speaking the word." I did not have a "word" from an actual funeral; so I asked Charlie Parham to make one for me. Remember, he is the husband of Minerva Parham, who told me about Lillian Napier's hearing the band of angels. He had known Sis Sarah Stinson a long time and told me what he would have said if he had been asked. He spoke in a voice resonant and unhurried, that could have offered comfort to the grieving and joy to the faithful.*

Rest On, Sis Sarah

Congregation: the young and the old: the Spirit has moved me to have a word to speak according to the life of Sister Sarah Stinson. And when a person is going to speak a thing

85

that is benefitable, I feel that one and all has the right to be quiet and pay heed to the word.

Sis Sarah has lived a good life and she has been dutiful to her churches; she has been a lamp in the darkness and a friend to the poor. And I know that Sis Sarah is a-resting from her labor today and that her works do follow her. We loved Sis Sarah, we did, and we miss the presence of her because she has been so dutiful.

But, Blessed Jesus, Sister Sarah has done gone on, and I know that she was ready to meet the Lord in peace. She has taken the wings of the morning and flew to her happy resting place.

Rest on, Sis Sarah, rest on.

Charles: *What kind of rhythm was it in?*

Rose: *A kind of minor cadence.*

Charles: *I know what a minor key is and what cadence is, but what is a minor cadence?*

Rose: *To me "minor cadence" means a sound of inherited sadness, maybe from slavery days: a minor key and a slowed cadence. Now a different kind of rhythm is in "An' She Didn't Get Tired." That is a funeral sermon. Aunt Orphelina Gentry was old and had died in Atlanta, but her body was brought back to White Plains for the funeral in the Second Baptist Church of White Plains. Aunt Orphelina had been born a Chester. An old woman who had known the Gentrys a long time and who had gone to the funeral recreated it for me. You should notice the rhythmic responses of the congregation and the quickening pace as it gets to the third line from the end, where it falls into a quiet anticlimax.*

Charlie Parham

An' She Didn't Get Tired

Aunt Orphelina done gone to her rest.
>*Do, Jesus!*

Ole Orphelina done slept away in death.
>*Umm-m-m . . . Save us, Jesus!*

But, howsomever it be, I see the hand of the Lord in that.
>*Um-m-m . . . Yes, Lord!*

Now I tell you, brethren:
I've seen the moon as it rose in the East
An' traveled beyond the western mountain.
>*Um-m-m-m . . . Yes, Lord!*

An' the earth, it go round an' round.
>*Um-m-m-m . . . Yes, Sweet Jesus!*

An' I see the hand of the Lord in that. . . .
>*Um-m-m . . . Yes, Lord!*

But, Ole Orphelina outshine 'em all.
>*Um-m-m-m . . . Yes, Lord!*

Just like the bright morning star,
Aunt Orphelina outshine them all;
For she done serve the Lord for
Eighty long years.
>*Um-m-m . . . Come, Sweet Jesus.*

And the beauty of it was,
She didn't git tired—
>*Um-m-m, Yes, Lord,*
>*She didn't git tired.*
>*An' she didn't git tired.*

Now, us all's seen the snow come driftin' down.
>*Um-m-m . . . Save us, Jesus!*

An' the pictures out of frost on the windowpane,
        Um-m-m . . . Yes, Lord!
An' I seen the hand of the Lord in that. . . .
        Um-m-m . . . Yes, Lord!
But, Sis Orphelina more gloryful than these,
For she done serve the Lord for eighty long years.
        Um-m-m . . . Save us, Sweet Jesus!
And the beauty of it was, she didn't git tired.
        Um-m-m . . . Yes, Lord!
        She didn't git tired . . .
        An' she didn't git tired.
Now, the lilies of the field . . .
        Um-m-m . . . Yes, Lord!
They didn't toil nor spin—
        Um-m-m . . . Yes, Sweet Jesus!
        Save us, Jesus!
But Sis Orphelina was—
She was more gloryful than these.
        Yes, Lord! . . . Um-m-m . . .
        Yes, My Lord!
Sis Orphelina was more gloryful than these.
        Um-m-m . . . Do, Sweet Jesus!
For she work, and she spun,
An' she raise her brood. . . .
She visit the poor and them that was lame. . . .
        True, Lord! . . . Do, Jesus!
And the beauty, and the glory of it was
She didn't git tired.
        Um-m-m . . . Yes, Lord! She didn't git,
        An' she didn't git tired.

Lillian Napier

Rose: *When I lived in Baldwin County, I asked someone whether he knew a good black preacher of the old school and was told that the Reverend James Sanders had the reputation of having been the best around there but that he was old and sick. I went to see him. I asked his wife if he felt like talking to me. She said yes, so I made arrangements. He set the day and said he would preach me a pulpit sermon. When I went back he was propped up on such white pillows, I remember. This was in the early 1940s down towards the settlement of Coopers. He was almost ninety. His mind was alert and he preached a wonderful sermon. He was a little man then, but he still had a rich voice, which he used almost like a musical*

90

instrument, strong cadences. I had my little homemade short-hand scheme and I got it all down. He went slow, but not too slow; he knew that I was taking it down. I had to go right home and get my initials and dashes all stretched out into words before I forgot.

Sound the Trumpet

When Jesus was here once on a time,
He left and He left in a cloud,
And He said that in like manner, the
World would see Him come again:
To select His jury—to collect up His peoples.
And that's what I see, that's what I see:
The Lord done come down in His chariot,
And done brought along a host of angels
for to help judge the world:
And brought Gabriel with Him to sound
the trumpet—to wake up the dead.
Chariot too holy to set on the ground—
Done stop it up there in mid-air,
And the Lord say to Gabriel to blow the
trumpet calm and easy,
For His peoples are not hard to wake—
Then Gabriel blew the trumpet calm and easy,
And the grave give way and the saints come up out of the
    ground,

Get up on top of the grave—stop and redress—
Pull off mortal and put on immortality,
Dress up now to get up on the chariot
That which Christ come down in.
Step up on the chariot, and Christ give orders for it to start
    back on high.
Then the chariot began to leave the earth
Going back on to heaven
And the watchman at the gate look out and see a crowd and
    say:
        I see a host coming all dressed in white—
        Who's them all coming all dressed in white?
And the word is going to be answered:
        These are they that have washed their robes
        And made them white in the blood of the Lamb.
By that time, the watchman will see the host a coming nigh
    and will say:
        Fly wide, Everlasting Gates,
        And let the purchase of my blood come in!
Then, when all the saints get there, they will go marching in.
And God will say to his servant:
        Look in the wardrobe and get the best robes and put
        on them—because they've been wearing garments
        that were secondhand.
And as they go marching in, they put rings on their fingers
    and palms of victory in their hands.
And I see all the saints marching in,
And they sit down at God's right hand;
And they join and sing the Hallelujah Song.

93

Epilogue

We are fortunate that Rose Thompson had the foresight and curiosity and love to seek out these stories and write them down. One morning when Rose was boarding with Miss Catherine Scott in Milledgeville, Mattie, who worked for Miss Scott, asked Rose, "Did you go over to Aunt Jane's house and get her to sing some old slavery songs to you?" Rose confessed she had. "Well, she done shouted in church about it," Mattie said, "and that started everybody getting up and telling their experiences back then and how hard the times were. Well, Aunt Jane got up and she tells about the white lady who came to see her and asked her to sing those old slavery songs. Jane said, 'The Lord done sent her there to get folks to singing the good old songs again.'" But Mattie got up in church to correct Aunt Jane: "No, it weren't the Lord; it were just Miss Rose."

It was just Miss Rose.